FINAL DIARIES

✺

FINAL DIARIES

✻

KELL CONNOR

NEW MICHIGAN PRESS
TUCSON, ARIZONA

NEW MICHIGAN PRESS
DEPT OF ENGLISH, P. O. BOX 210067
UNIVERSITY OF ARIZONA
TUCSON, AZ 85721-0067

<http://newmichiganpress.com>

Orders and queries to <nmp@thediagram.com>.

Copyright © 2021 by Kell Connor.
All rights reserved.

ISBN 978-1-934832-79-0. FIRST PRINTING.

Design by Ander Monson.

Cover image by the author.

CONTENTS

The Double Daughter   1
A Note on the Lake   2
The Death of the Double Daughter   3
At the Bottom of the Sound of Women Weeping   4
A Note on the Double Daughter's Vocabulary and Language Skills   5
Her New Name   6
The Triple Clown's Ongoing Troubles   7
The Triple Clown's Constant Revelations   8
and Her Hands   9
(Whoever She Is) Considers the Water Anew   10
For Those Who Wonder if She is Capable of Arson   11
The Quadruple Arcangel   12
The Please   13
Whomsoever and How Many of Her Final Diaries   14
A Note on the Final Diaries   15
An Incomplete History of Her Sorrows   16
Special Diet   17
How Is Her Appetites?   18
The Forest Beneath the Forest Before Her   19
The Workweek Beneath Each of Her Day   20
The Horses   13
A Note on the Landscape   22
The Octopus   23
A Note on the Octopus   24
Index   25

THE DOUBLE DAUGHTER

There were seven daughters each given to a different form of daughterhood. The double daughter was the only child conscribed to be the steward of her own delight. She was appraised as a prize in the eyes of men, and she was seized by constraints that tightened like slipknots as she shifted within her discomfort. When it was time to wed, she took the lake into her bed, pail by pail, minnows in death throes atop the softness of her worn comforter. The fishes' skittish iridescence was more like light's residue than light's resonance, but she began to chart her circular course by those flashes as though they were constant stars. Her stars were displaced by the sunrise, the room rinsed with clear light. Her bed was swollen with lakewater and littered with cold fish. Nothing was ruined: She had drawn in her diary a detailed map.

A NOTE ON THE LAKE

She had heard about women drowning. It happened often. Her six sisters, for example, were all at the bottom of the lake. There was an element of glamour to it, making the contaminated lake a permanent address. Like being sewn into a costly gown, or contracting blood poisoning from a poorly pinned corsage. The body of water that formed the border of the double daughter's ghostly town was commonly known as the Sound of Women Weeping. It was well-stocked with scavengers, mostly catfish, and a lone octopus whose singular intelligence was sensed as a soft vibration by every diver, including those who never surfaced.

THE DEATH OF THE DOUBLE DAUGHTER

On the morning of her drowning, the double daughter fills her pockets with fishhooks. As her last act on land she chooses to use one, impaling a baitfish with great care, hook threaded through the skin above the spine. This spares the minnow's life. The call of the lure is not the fact of the body but the little bit of fight left in it. She loves the gulping thump of the water breaking as the fish hits, as though she'd thrown a stone too large to skip on the surface, but too small to sink her. She declined to tie the hook to a line, so the fish is permitted some terrible freedom. She isn't sure if her last act on land is an example of cruelty or of cowardice, but she begins to understand the things a false mercy might be disguised as, and decides at once that she will not rush to meet her death. She will walk alongside it slowly, sworn to carry its sign.

AT THE BOTTOM OF THE SOUND OF WOMEN WEEPING

The double daughter's discoveries don't prevent her from diving. A few leagues below the surface, she does hear a kind of feminine keening. But the sonic effect is dislocated, the way sobbing sounds inside the skull of a girl crying. Damp gasping, an iris bulb slipping down the throat. Weeping isn't passive, it is a form of erosion revealing secret recesses. Often the reason a woman is crying is that she is angry. Often the reason a woman is angry is that she must weep so often and so deeply. The double daughter understands: She never wanted to drown, but it seemed like she needed to die so often. She can't locate the octopus, but she finds lush plantlife on the lakebed, soft, esophageal, soundless. *A sarcaphogus of luse,* she writes later in her diary, her meaning either obscured or expressed in perfect encryption by her poor spelling or pure invention.

A NOTE ON THE DOUBLE DAUGHTER'S VOCABULARY AND LANGUAGE SKILLS

The double daughter is a dropout. She didn't even finish kindergarten. Where did she learn the word *sarcophagus* and how does she know how to spell it correctly? It's not that mysterious, really: She has a book about the construction of the Egyptian pyramids that she shoplifted from the thrift store. She acquires language like a kleptomaniac, a word like a tube of lipstick slipped swiftly into her hip pocket. Sometimes she loves a word so much she practices it on the mirror in the morning with lipstick, or with her index finger in the gathered steam after her shower. Sarcophagus. This is her only consistent religious practice, so she does make an effort to mimic the order of the letters precisely.

HER NEW NAME

A minor alteration changes everything: daughter becomes laughter after cleaving the curve of the D, and Double Laughter bounces off the walls, like an echo or a superball, leaving little bruises. *henforth, I am known to me as Triple Clown*

THE TRIPLE CLOWN'S ONGOING TROUBLES

Being at a loss, always, like a second adolescence, slicing lemons in the kitchen alone. In order to reach an understanding of the nature of love, she listens repeatedly to Diana Ross and the Supremes singing "Someday We'll Be Together," but the record is playing too slowly, the turntable set at the wrong speed, the 45 spinning at 33. It sounds mournful, as love does under time's distortion. *I never know quiet how to make any thing go at its propr speed,* she writes. It's true she was born into a kind of slowness, a horse who shirks the saddle, longing to remain as close as possible to stillness, all movements matched to the pace of pasture's ambling flatness. The song isn't better this way, but the way the clarion Motown vocals are pulled into low, ominous gospel, unnaturally masculine, might eventually offer her greater revelations. The triple clown receives revelation upon revelation, but she rarely receives any relief.

THE TRIPLE CLOWN'S CONSTANT REVELATIONS

I must be at least as voilent as this world, she writes. Is a veil a kind of violence against the visible? Her eyes mired in mirrors, the slime of admiration. It's uncertain if there's such a thing as the unadorned self, but perhaps that uncanny moment when a face is displaced by a sudden lack of mask comes closest. She often writes *closets* to mean *closest*, but always writes *the walls are closing in* when she goes in the closet to hide. She keeps her usual clothing in a pile on the floor, so the triple clown's little closet only contains the things she never wears, empty of her on their hangers. She could be a different person if she wasn't already living several other lives.

AND HER HANDS

I dont know what Im spose to do, she writes. She means with her hands. How many of them are her? Or were there? There are things she needs to see in person, and things she needs to touch in theory. The visible isn't always a viable option. She believes glass is the true material of the soul, cool and translucent, produced by compression, the sand of the banks of the lake blasted into coherence and clarity. Her task is not to see things clearly, but to see through them once the world has forcibly assembled them. Loss compressed into something like love, its gloss at least as magnifying as a spyglass. Light becomes a blazing pinpoint capable of incinerating all it falls upon, and all things seem nearer to her. None of this solves the problem of what to do with her hands.

(WHOEVER SHE IS) CONSIDERS THE WATER ANEW

There is a type of repetition that reveals more than its own pattern. The daughter's doubling over into laughter and then triangulating into a fatherless jester is a particularly troubling example. She covers the mirrors in her home with a thick mist harvested from the surface of the lake in early morning. This protects her from the pattern she's a part of, but leaves her lonesome as a goldfish in a small bowl. *I focus on the wrong feelling,* she writes. She can think of herself as *lonely*, or she can think of herself as *floating*. Are those the only options? *I think too much of water,* she writes and crosses out. She means she needs to remember the rocks below.

FOR THOSE WHO WONDER IF SHE IS CAPABLE OF ARSON

She would do it gently. There is a type of symmetry only achievable by a skilled lacemaker or a controlled burn. The crenellated edges of the house's foundation after the fire, the fine patterns of char on the few remaining roofbeams, ashes settling into previously invisible crevices. Destruction often functions as a forceful emphasis on the essence of a structure. Like all enduring knowledge, this arrives too late to be truly useful. The firehose leaves the scraps of blankets frozen into brittle slabs. *My sadness are most only weariness*, she writes. It follows that she'll find a kind of happiness when she curls up like a cat and sleeps within whatever warmth remains in the rubble.

THE QUADRUPLE ARCANGEL

Softness in skeins: the skin of the air against hers. There's no cure for the new fever but the cooler water of the lake's lower layer might help a little. She won't go to the shore today. Hell's a world within a world, a willingness where she slips past simple possibility into sure thing, thrown stone, a window shattered for the sheer sound of it. *my true love is Vandalsm,* she writes. The dark tries to adjust to her eyes. She's not well. A wet cough in an empty cathedral belongs to the things of this world, but its echo answers elsewhere. *the paradice Ive been promised is unbarable,* she writes in her best handwriting.

THE PLEASE

Her illness is inhospitable to metaphor so she abandons all attempts at description. Her prescriptions seem encrypted, the syllables existing outside of common language: Trademarked names. Her inkwell is dwindling, her indwelling spirit wavering. She's sick with shame, which means she's cured in a bad way, preserved by salt, dried out. She doesn't die but death is her companion and her comfort, like the hum from the oscillating fan. *Something soft to fall sleep to,* she writes. She is visited by a series of sisterly shadows, not presences exactly, more like passages into the past. *The past happnd so fast,* she writes. She blinks slowly, missing it again.

WHOMSOEVER AND HOW MANY OF HER FINAL DIARIES

Her final diaries are more attentive to the weather. *theres a choice of rain*, she writes, or *a thick Snows forecast*. She only considers the predicted weather, never what actually happens. She also omits the way in which the light was changing. The light had taken on a taste and texture. It was pallid and oily like a smear of butter at room temperature. The light had also begun to make sounds, a hum as it hit the ground, a crackle like static as it passed through the kitchen window or navigated the spaces between oak leaves. *What if miricles are normal but we forgot*, she writes, perhaps in reference to the light, meaning its new properties seemed divine. She writes very little, almost nothing, but her final diaries do not feel unfinished. They have a sheen of silence, intact and fixed, that seals her to the spare text. The pages swell with her worldlessness like waves, whitecaps of blankness that bear her forward, a spitting likeness.

A NOTE ON THE FINAL DIARIES

The phrase *final diaries* may be misleading, as it refers to all of her diaries, even the earliest, and, as always, our darling does not die. Her diaries remain ongoing. The finality refers to a cessation of self where there's something else rushing in to replace it. The lacy froth at the cusp of the surf. She was scared the first time she saw it, sure that the lake would not stop advancing and the shore she stood upon would shortly vanish. The water did overtake her, but not in the fashion she imagined. It was like a kiss emptied perfectly of any context, neither sweet nor sinister, just a gesture dissolving two perimeters into a single resemblance. *waking up feels the same as falling sleep so I cant choose between it*, she writes. "Final" here means she's willing to dwell in the deep wherever it deigns to meet her.

AN INCOMPLETE HISTORY OF HER SORROWS

She wanted to follow the path of the arrow, but she was made for water, not air. She wanted to learn a way to love the world more accurately, but she was made for faltering. For a long time, she thought of her limited memory as a nuisance, a minor chord played on the strings of a prior life. Then she thought her memory wasn't the resonating note but the tape hiss that began to mask the sound with static on each playback. Later, she thought her memory was only a crow that knows to go back to a field where it found food before. It seemed likely that appetite was what bound her to the past. Once she thought of her hunger as a haunting, it was harder to live with but hurt less, as if her memory was just a list of things she'd learn to live without. And so it is. The double daughter no longer requires the object of her desire. She only needs to keep its source as her central secret, a loadbearing wall for the house she will haunt but never inhabit. Again, her diaries are most important to us for what they omit.

SPECIAL DIET

It's very simple: Lemon, honey, hot water. She's heard that these things ward off soreness, somehow. *nothing heals as well as ones own patientce*, she writes, meaning the balm is in the time she spends waiting for the water to cool down enough to drink. Sometimes she scalds her mouth in haste and hunger, and then both the sweetness and the sourness vanish, replaced by brief pain and enduring numbness. She's never liked salt, considers it the province of the deer and horses, pressing their noses to huge cubes of sodium. It seems like a gesture of reverence, their necks bent so gently, but it's only instinct recognizing a necessary nutrient. Is there something saline she could approach as a supplicant? *a block of the solid materal of tears*, she writes, *that I cold lick and I wold not cry anmore.* She has concerns that her frequent weeping is a poor use of her time.

HOW IS HER APPETITES?

She can taste that the honey was made by bees' bodies. It's subtle, something just shy of decay, complicated and acrid. The lemon's astringency rinses it away, so she often takes a spoonful of honey unaccompanied. At formal dinners she claims to have no appetite, but this is because she can't bear to eat the steaming roasts placed before her. A calf, a duck, a pig, a lamb: *they eat the animals I wold speak to*, she writes, sucking her spoon clean. If the honey is exceptionally sweet, she knows it will crystallize sooner. She sometimes senses a similar granulation happening inside her mind, her liquid thoughts thickening into multifaceted candies. *Im becoming a confeccsion*, she writes. So the state she's in is sweetness to her, always.

THE FOREST BENEATH THE FOREST BEFORE HER

Shadows, spruce branches loosen the light and reduce her. A slow shimmer thickens and sweetens even further; she clings to the back of the spoon. The woods warp and wrap around her. Damp spring, sharp chirps, shrapnel. She sings with her mouth shut so it must be sonar. Death arrives disguised as renewal, ash trees processed into polished caskets. What she asks for matters more than what she has been given. And what does she ask for? *I want to go to a empty-out stable and sleep in hay on the flor.* She's never wanted a home, only a suitable habitat. Neither pure wilderness nor strict confinement. The house once felt like a nice place to hide, but she knows it holds horrors. The forest holds her and wards off all of indoors, but she's set on the stables, the fortress the horses' absence would form.

THE WORKWEEK BENEATH EACH OF HER DAY

Her days seem the same, rinsing her hair strand by strand. Life's a dream in the sense that it's reoccurring, beyond that it's too uselessly lucid to qualify as dream. There's also a similar rate of attrition in terms of memory, which is one reason for the diary. *I shold memorise ten minutes of each the day before its turnt away from my mind*, she writes. Impossible. It's not that nowhere is safe, just that nowhere is more safe than anywhere else. At this time the diaries begin to focus almost entirely on descriptions of the sky.

THE HORSES

The day curdles into night. The horses are more than the sum of their saddles. Past the paddock, past the pasture, an interlocking thicket of roses. Their whinnies peel the air away. The name of the town means "to scatter," and it's lovely to say aloud: Ogallala, stolen land. The double daughter witnesses from a distance the horses on the highway, blocking traffic. The double daughter loves it, an equestrian trespass, the world suspended in a thickening aspic. She knows she'll be in trouble for letting the horses out, but she doesn't know with whom. *forgiviness is the fog of law*, she writes, feeling the weight of the word in her writing hand and in her jaw, as if forgiveness were what she'd been asking for all along.

A NOTE ON THE LANDSCAPE

It's nothing, really. There's the horizon, a perfectly flat line where the eye can rest while the self becomes unfocused. The world a block of text she no longer needs to read, having memorized the information long ago. Her mind is free to follow a hawk so precisely that the secret of flight is revealed. A type of soaring propelled by the counterweight of boredom. She's become so used to sustaining this particular equilibrium that she cannot reasonably expect to survive elsewhere if she were to leave. The idea of a crowded sidewalk! *I wold rather be lonesome than earthbounned*, she writes.

THE OCTOPUS

A tangled octopus can camouflage to match the net that traps her. She knows she can't actually hide from her captivity, but the response is emotive rather than strictly tactical, a complex gesture toward the idea of freedom. Mimicry and masquerade are common defensive techniques, but they risk eroding the distinction between the captive and the state-of-captivity. It's happening already, creating a vapor lock in the water that alters the patterns of the waves. On the shore the double daughter senses something is wrong but blames her own perception. *Harms way is my hole lanscape*, she writes.

A NOTE ON THE OCTOPUS

It is impossible for an octopus to live in a freshwater lake. However, many miracles are unintelligible to us. There is also the possibility of mythology, a cryptid invented to sell souvenirs or lure tourists who will trawl the lake looking for her. This explains the net, too. Someone has named the octopus Monstrous Esmerelda. The double daughter shoplifts a magnet from the Gas N Shop that says *I SWAM WITH MONSTROUS ESMERELDA* in script meant to resemble tentacles. Is it still considered a souvenir if she uses it to remind herself of a place she'll never leave? *Yes there is a octpus*, she writes. *but im not sure if what her REAL name is.* She underlines *REAL* with a set of emphatic parallel lines, traced and retraced until their impression is perceptible throughout the few remaining pages in her diary.

INDEX

Sharp air. Marigold, the scent of the other world, the underworld, on a clear day. Lilac, soft red wheat. She will miss it: The carnal, that char of desire. That bitter register, the marigolds again, the color of cartoon flames. Body heat trapped beneath a worn quilt. *I go into the next room and its the same room repeatd*, she writes. That's the softness of this world, or all she can know of it. It's as fragile as foam. Where her form ends something else begins in the warm air. *or I go into the next room and its the same room repeatd*, she writes. It feels like receding, like something sneaking away and then coming right back through a different door. At a certain point a sense of place just assembles from thin air. *I am inside my arrival*, she writes. And here the phrases begin to fall apart at all points, too tender for our grammar.

KELL CONNOR lives in Nebraska. Their work appears in *Bennington Review, Berkeley Poetry Review, Columbia Poetry Review,* and elsewhere. They are the author of the chapbook *For Destruction* (Doomtown Records USA, 2018).

❋

COLOPHON

Text is set in a digital version of Jenson, designed by Robert Slimbach in 1996, and based on the work of punchcutter, printer, and publisher Nicolas Jenson. The titles here are in Futura.

❊

NEW MICHIGAN PRESS, based in Tucson, Arizona, prints poetry and prose chapbooks, especially work that transcends traditional genre. Together with DIAGRAM, NMP sponsors a yearly chapbook competition.

DIAGRAM, a journal of text, art, and schematic, is published bimonthly at THEDIAGRAM.COM. Periodic print anthologies are available from the New Michigan Press at NEWMICHIGANPRESS.COM.

www.ingramcontent.com/pod-product-compliance
Lightning Source LLC
Chambersburg PA
CBHW031507040426
42444CB00007B/1247